IMAGES OF ENGLAND

BLYTH

Matthew Tate – The pitman's Poet Laureate, known as 'Auld Matti' to his pitman friends. Born at Benton Square in 1837 he started working in the mines at the age of twelve for the sum of 10d (4p) a day. He never had a serious accident but personally knew of several, including the Hartley Pit Disaster of 1862. A keen supporter of every movement designed to benefit the workers, he used his voice and pen to this end. He was a regular contributor to the *Blyth News & Wansbeck Telegraph* and had a number of books of poetry published. He retired at the age of seventy-six in 1913, and was presented with a house in Queens Lane by Lord Ridley rent free for as long as he cared to occupy it. Matthew died in this house at the age of eighty-four in October 1920.

IMAGES OF ENGLAND

BLYTH

BLYTH LOCAL STUDIES GROUP

EDITED BY BOB BALMER

PHOTOGRAPHIC WORK BY
DAVE DURWARD & ELDRED ROUTLEDGE

The
History
Press

Blyth Grammar School Sixth Form, Summer 1941. Left to right: Lucy Proom, Jean Ferrel, Vera Johnson, Joan Parnaby, Nora Appleby, Moira Forster, Derek Hood, Ronald Dodds, Hugh Steel, Raymond Wilson and Jim Pace.

First published in 1997 by Tempus Publishing
Reprinted 1998, 2001, 2002, 2005

Reprinted in 2008 by
The History Press
The Mill, Brimscombe Port,
Stroud, Gloucestershire, GL5 2QG
www.thehistorypress.co.uk

British Library Cataloguing in Publication Data.
A catalogue record for this book is available from the British Library.

ISBN 978 0 7524 0773 9

Typesetting and origination by
Tempus Publishing Limited.
Printed and bound in England.

Contents

Snow clearing at Blyth, 19 November 1962. The church and the shops on the far side of the road have all gone now and the area is now covered by the Keel Row shopping mall.

Acknowledgements

Thanks must go to all those people, too numerous to mention by name, who over the years have contributed background information to many of the photographs used in this book. Thanks must also go to Mr Andrew Clark of Chalford Publishing for his technical help with this book and to Ms Angela Johnstone for proof reading the book.

Acknowledgement is given to the following for the use of photographs in the book:
Blyth Local History Society, Blyth Resource & Initiative Centre, North East Press Ltd,
Mr Thomas S. Allen, Miss Connie Atkinson, Miss Joyce Carlisle, Mr Eddie Cain,
Mr John Herron (Bebside), Mr John Herron (Blyth), Mr Jim Pace, Mr Hughe Patterson,
Mr Douglas Pearson, Mr Gordon Smith.

NOTE
While every effort has been made to ensure the accuracy of the text the Blyth Local Studies Group would like to hear from anyone who may have further information about photographs in the book. If anyone has old photographs of interest which can be used in other publications the Group would like to hear from you by contacting:

Blyth Local Studies Group
c/o 95 Disraeli Street
Blyth NE24 1JB.

Introduction

The contemporary view of Blyth is of an industrial town with little or no roots other than the coal trade. This may well have been true for the far distant past, but during the last two hundred years other industries have been and gone, and left their mark.

To understand the history of the present township of Blyth one must first look at the history of Newsham and Cowpen, both of which had a greater importance than Blyth at one time. Newsham having habitation sites dating from the Romano-British period, while between Bebside Village and Bebside Hall there is a large Saxon settlement.

The Church played a major role in the early mining and fishing history of the area; Tynemouth Priory for the Newsham estates, Newminster Abbey near Morpeth for the Cowpen estates and the Bishop of Durham for the north side of the river, as Bedlingtonshire was a detached portion of the County Palatine of Durham until 1844 when the Detached Counties Act was passed.

When one looks at the present township of Blyth it is inconceivable to think that only one hundred and twenty-five years ago more than eighty per cent of the area was green fields.

The history of the port and town of Blyth as we know it can be said to date from the year 1723. On the 11 July of that year the Lordship of Newsham was put up for sale by the Commissioners of Forfeited Estates at their office in the Inner Temple, London. The Newsham Estate had been the property of Thomas Ratcliffe, the Earl of Derwentwater, and had been forfeited to the crown because he was on the wrong side during the 1715 'Jacobite Rising'.

The estate was purchased by Matthew White, a merchant adventurer, of Newcastle and his son-in-law Richard Ridley and it was under these two men that the first new quays and houses were built on the south side of the river.

The history of the port dates from the twelfth century, but all that development took place on the north side of the river under the Bishop of Durham. Although the development of the port from 1723 was a continuous thing two major dates in its development were 1854 when the Blyth Harbour & Docks Board was formed, and 1882 when the Blyth Harbour Commission was formed.

During the twentieth century, until it closed in 1967, Blyth shipbuilding yard was known as the 'Largest Shipyard on the North-East Coast' having five dry docks and five building berths all in one yard and having over half a mile of river frontage.

The port reached its peak as a coal shipping port by the early 1960s, shipping over six million tons a year. But the decline started with the closure of the railway into Blyth in 1965 (1964 for passenger traffic). This was followed by a steady closure of collieries in south-east Northumberland, so by the beginning of the 1980s the only coal staiths left were the West Staiths and the port was a shadow of its former-self.

The town of Blyth as we know it also starts to develop from 1723, although before that date there was the Nook Farm and one or two fishermen's cottages near the quayside area. The major dates in the development of the town are from 1723 and 1815 for the older parts.

Work started on the development of the Cowpen Quay area in 1810 and the Waterloo area after 1815. In both areas there was a large increase in house building after the 1850s. During the 1890s there was a large amount of rebuilding in the older part of the town.

The 1920s and '30s saw the development of new housing estates on the outskirts of the expanding town. The next and last major housing developments around Blyth took place from the 1950s to '70s.

In 1863 the South Blyth Local Board was formed which took over the duties of the Parish Council for the day to day running of the town. At this time Blyth was part of the Parish of Earsdon. The Cowpen Local Board was formed in 1864, taking over from the Parish Council which met at Horton Church.

Under the Local Government Act of 1894 both Local Boards became Urban District Councils, and in 1906 they were amalgamated to form the Blyth Urban District Council. With the passing of a Parliamentary Act the Blyth Municipal Borough Council came into being on the 21 September 1922. By this time Bebside was also part of the Borough.

The year 1935 saw the southern boundary of the Borough moved from Meggies Burn to Seaton Burn, which took in part of Seaton Sluice and Seaton Delaval Hall. With the reorganisation of boundaries in 1974 Blyth Valley Borough Council was formed from the amalgamation of Blyth Municipal Borough, Seaton Valley Urban District and Cramlington Urban District Councils.

Throughout most of the one hundred years of history we are looking at in the photographs, employment in the Blyth area had always been male dominated heavy industries such as fishing, foundry work, shipping, shipbuilding, shipbreaking, mining and railways. But with the closure of the railway, the shipyard, the pits and Battleship Wharf, by the mid 1980s the employment of the town had changed to female dominated light industries such as the clothing, electrical industry and others, all of which have factories on the Blyth and Kitty Brewster Industrial Trading Estates.

Bob Balmer
Blyth Local Studies Group

One

In and Around Blyth
Blyth, Bebside, Cowpen, Newsham, New Delaval and Cambois

Belgrave Crescent, *c.* 1910. Note the height of the trees in Ridley Park on the right hand side.

Baths House in Bath Terrace built in the 1780s. These public baths were advertised in the early nineteenth century as Hot, Cold and Vapour Baths. The building is now a private residence.

The High Light in the back lane behind Bath Terrace. The lower half dates from 1788. The structure was heightened twice, first in the mid 1820s and again in 1896 after the South Harbour was built. This light was in use until the 1980s when it was replaced by another nearer the river.

The Ridley Arms, built in 1788 as a private house for George Marshall a local shipowner and ropemaker. It became a public house in the early nineteenth century. The licence transferred to the Sea Horse Hotel on the 6 May 1966 and the building was demolished in 1968.

Northumberland Street, c. 1900, showing the then newly rebuilt Star & Garter Hotel and the Kings Head Hotel on the right hand side of the street.

STAR & GARTER HOTEL
(*Family and Commercial*) BLYTH

A.A. Hotel.   Fully Licensed.   Moderate Tariff
Excellent Cuisine. Every Accommodation for visitors
GOOD GARAGE   LUNCHEONS DAILY

Star & Garter Hotel advert, *c.* 1920, but the picture is much earlier.

Alderman John Dent, *c.* 1895. Born in 1845, he was a native of Blyth and a well-known shipowner. He was head of the firm of Dent & Co. of Newcastle & Blyth and also a director of Blyth Shipbuilding Co. Ltd. He was a member of Blyth Harbour Commission, Senior Magistrate at Blyth, a member of the North of England Steamship Federation, Chairman of the Northumberland Fisheries Committee, Ruling Councillor of Blyth Habitation of the Primrose League, President of Blyth Constitutional Club, President of Blyth Spartans FC, and associated with many other public organisations in Blyth. Alderman Dent died in 1907.

Sea View, *c.* 1910, originally the old Custom House, it later became the offices for the Engineers Staff of the Harbour Commissioners.

The Old Chapel of Ease at Blyth built in 1751, the first place of worship to be built at Blyth. St Cuthbert's church hall now stands on the site of the Old Chapel.

St Cuthbert's church as it looked in 1885 when only part completed. The old Chapel of Ease can be seen on the right.

St Cuthbert's church from the south-east as it was in the early 1930s.

The old Ebeneezer chapel and school, built in 1814 at a cost of £270. It was used as a church for sixty years, then became the home for the Scientific Institute until it was demolished to make way for the present police station in 1894.

Market Street, c. 1870 – now part of Plessey Road, from Blagdon Street (now Bridge Street) to Sussex Street. Akenhead's shop later became Swalwell's shop, now the site of the Harbour Commission Offices.

The first Blyth Police Station was built in 1860 at a cost of £150 with £30 extra for furniture. This building was situated on the corner of Eldon Street and Carlton Street. It was in use for thirty-six years until the present police station was opened in 1896.

In 1894 it was decided to build a new Police Station and Law Courts at a cost of £11,900. This large imposing building was opened in 1896 and the station is still in use today over 100 years later.

The bunkering berth and houses on the High Quay near the Lord Nelson Inn, locally known as the 'Dock House' and 'Nelson Place', c. 1920.

Blyth & Tyne Brewery built in 1784, was a brewery until 1916. It was known as the Brewery Bar and is now the Boat House Tavern.

Blyth's third post office built in 1860. This shop front still looks the same today more than 130 years later.

Blyth's fourth post office built in 1893 on the corner of Plessey Road and Carlton Street. This building later became the local employment exchange.

Plessey Road Mixed School in the mid 1960s. This school was opened on the 5 December 1892 by Mr J.B. Forster JP and had cost £5,275 to build.

Plessey Road Mixed School, Group 6, 1919-20. The male teacher is Mr Aquila Forster who was at this school for many years.

A painting of the second Waterloo Bridge built in 1841. The estimated cost for the first Waterloo Bridge, built around 1815 for the Morpeth to North Shields Turnpike Trust, was £30. Albion House was built by J. & W. Simpson on this site during 1895-97.

Waterloo Bridge just before it was removed in the early 1890s. The area to the right of this picture was Wright's timber yard which later became the bus station.

The north end of Beaconsfield Street, *c.* 1900. The building on the right is Albion House the property of Hedley & Company.

Hedley, Young's Albion House advertisement, *c.* 1931.

G. & N. Wright's timber yard, Bridge Street, c. 1900. This site is now covered by the bus station and the main post office.

The east end of Waterloo Road. This photograph dates from the mid 1890s. The Central Hall was built in 1858 and J. Hepworth & Son, Outfitters, opened their shop there in 1896.

The Market Place corner, *c.* 1895. The framework with the theatre sign was one of the early electric street lamps. They did not last for long because they were too high and the light was not strong enough.

The Town Clerk reading the Royal Charter, granted on the 21 September 1922, in the Market Place. It proclaimed Blyth a Municipal Corporation on the 9 November 1922.

Market Day, *c.* 1900. Note the wood stalls and some of the items for sale laid out on the ground.

Market Day, *c.* 1960.

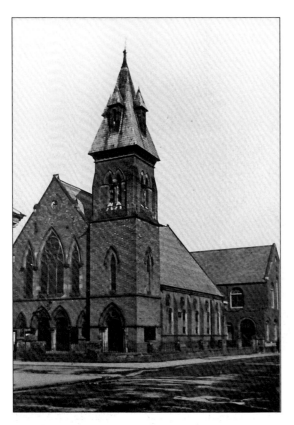

The Methodist Zion church, Waterloo Road, cost £2,200 to build and was opened on the 6 September 1864. This photograph shows the church pre-1939, as the spire was damaged and the top removed during the Second World War.

St Mary's church at the west end of the Market Place, cost £1,600 to build and was opened on the 14 June 1864. Further extensions were made to the church in 1896 when St Mary's became the main church for the Parish of Cowpen.

The Catholic church of Our Lady and St Wilfrid, on Waterloo Road, was built in 1863 and for a little more than 100 years was served by priests of the English Benedictine Congregation.

In June 1961 the oldest Roman Catholic priest in the country, ninety-six year old Father James Oswald Hall of St Wilfrid's, Blyth, celebrated seventy years of priesthood.

The English Presbyterian church at the west end of Waterloo Road, built at a cost of £5,000, was opened on the 6 June 1876. The large building on the left of the church was added in 1893 as the new church hall and Sunday school.

Turner Street, *c*. 1910. The 'White Shop' was built next to the Railway Hotel, now the Pullman, after three shops had been destroyed by fire in 1904.

The Blyth Urban District Council Offices in Seaforth Street, off Turner Street, *c.* 1912. Built in the late 1860s as Cowpen Local Board Offices they continued as the Cowpen U.D.C. Offices until 1906 when the Cowpen and Blyth Councils amalgamated. The building was demolished in the early 1990s.

The Mayor's Parade from the Council Chambers in Seaforth Street passing along Regent Street (formerly Turner Street), 4 June 1967.

Regent Street, Cowpen Quay, looking north from the railway bridge, *c.* 1900. The four shops on the right is where Firstfreeze is situated now.

Front Street, Bebside, *c.* 1900. The Bebside Inn is on the left, with the road leading across the railway to Cowpen Lane.

The old timber railway bridge near Bedlington Iron Works, with the Rose & Crown public house in its shadow, *c.* 1900.

The entrance to what was locally known as the 'Half-penny Woods'. There used to be a toll of one half penny to walk through the Bebside woods along the south side of the river Blyth.

Cowpen Village near the Sidney Arms, *c.* 1890.

The road through Cowpen Village before it was altered, 8 August 1960.

Newsham Mechanics' Institute, built during the second half of 1896. The new workmen's institute was opened by Mr R.E. Ornsby on the 20 February 1897. After a long and checkered life it was burnt down in 1994 when a furniture saleroom.

Newsham & New Delaval Co-operative Society started in 1864. This picture shows their shops in Elliott Street, Newsham. The building was burnt down around 1914 and later the Victory Club was built on the site.

Boca Chica, Cambois, 11 May 1970. Having provided homes for many generations, these old colliery rows are due for demolition. Note the old toilet and coal house across the street from the houses.

Mrs Nellie Cowell standing beside her old-fashioned 'Black Range' kitchen grate in her house at Boca Chica, Cambois, 11 May 1970.

Two

Shops

John Fraser's shop near the Market Place corner, known locally as 'The Wood Hut'. Here he published his own paper the *Blyth Scribe*, *c.* 1900.

William Soulsby's hat shop, *c*. 1880. This shop was situated on Waterloo Road, just to the east of Fraser's Wood Hut, between the 'hut' and the entrance to the old Theatre Royal.

Edward Soulsby the bakers, Bowes Street, *c*. 1880. The cart driver is Thomas Lee Soulsby, Edward's eldest son. The other four are also sons of Edward Soulsby.

Woodcock's shop in Church Street as it was in 1900. It first opened for business on Saturday 9 May 1896. The shop looked like this until some slight alterations were made to the shop front in 1934.

After seventy years in business this is how the shop looked on the 25 April 1966. Today after 100 years on the same site the shop has been modernised once again as they progress into a new century.

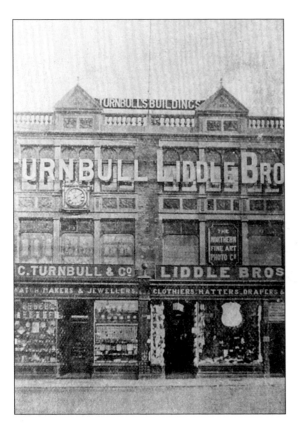

Cuthbert Turnbull's shop in Waterloo Road, *c.* 1895. This shop replaced an older one which was destroyed by fire on the 4 February 1890.

The staff in front of the London & Newcastle Tea Co. shop in Waterloo Road, *c.* 1885. Boots the chemists is now on this site.

George Cummings' shoe shop, Waterloo Road, *c.* 1895. Cummings had been a boot and shoe maker in the Blyth area from the 1840s. This building still stands today and is still a shoe shop, now owned by Robson's.

Robson Bros boot and shoe makers, *c.* 1910. This firm still sells boots and shoes to this day in the same shop in Waterloo Road.

I. Chapple, baker and grocers shop in Wellington Street, *c.* 1896. Left to right: master Thomas Chapple, John Good (manager), Isaac Chapple (owner), master's Joseph and Ernie Chapple. The cart driver is unknown.

Captain Laird with some of his staff in front of his shop in Bowes Street, *c.* 1920.

R.S. Atkinson's shop with Isabella Atkinson in the doorway, *c.* 1910. This shop was on the corner of Croft Road and Middleton Street.

William Ashby, butcher, standing in the doorway of his shop on Croft Road next door to Atkinson's, *c.* 1910. William is standing there looking more like a prize fighter than a butcher.

Blyth Co-operative Society main branch shop in Croft Road. Built in 1902 on the site of the first Tudor's Circus.

Blyth Co-operative Society, Marlow Street branch, at what was then Cowpen Colliery, c. 1960.

Waterloo Road, *c.* 1960, with the Electricity shop, C.A. Boast's clothing shop, the Co-op optician, the *Blyth News* office and the Co-op chemists. These buildings, except the Electricity shop, were all demolished for the building in the late 1960s of the Co-op's large 'Northumbria House'.

Waterloo Road, *c.* 1960. David Baron's shop is still the same, but Robert Soulsby's, the butchers, is now a bakers shop.

James Marshall, baker and confectioner, *c.* 1890. Upstairs was Marshall's Cafe. The shop was on Turner Street opposite the Market Place. This shop later became the Central Pork Shop.

Looking down Turner Street (now Regent Street) towards the Railway Station, *c.* 1900. The shop on the left is the Cash Boot Company.

From the ashes of the fire on the 26 October 1904 rose the large new 'White Shop' the property of Mr J.W. Chisholm in Turner Street.

Furniture Goodness has always been our aim.

All the LATEST DESIGNS in our SHOWROOMS.

DINING ROOM
Furniture

NOTE THE ADDRESS:

CHISHOLM'S
WHITE SHOP, BLYTH.
OPPOSITE THE STATION.

An advertisement for the White Shop, *c.* 1931.

John Mouat's Cowpen Quay Bazaar, established around 1880. It was situated on the corner of Maddison Street and Regent Street.

LAMPE VERITAS
50 AND 100 CANDLE-POWER.

FROM 10/6 UPWARDS, AT
JOHN MOUAT'S,
AGENT FOR BLYTH AND DISTRICT,
COMPLETE HOUSE FURNISHER,
REGENT ST. AND MADDISON ST.,
COWPEN QUAY, BLYTH.

An advert for oil lamps sold by John Mouat's from the *Blyth Examiner*, 1 March 1890.

One of the oldest, if not the oldest business in Blyth, run by the Herron family. Established in 1841 in Croft Street (now King Street), this picture shows their new shop in Regent Street around 1900.

Moses Taylor's general dealers shop and Archibold Ramsden's music shop on the north side of Regent Street around 1900. This site is now the Firstfreeze shop.

The sign may say 'Motor Insurance' but if you look closely at the pillars above the door and window you will see the shop had originally been a butchers shop. Carved on the pillars, left to right, are a pig's head, a ram's head and a beast's head.

Three

Leisure, Entertainment and Sport

Looking north along Blyth Beach, *c.* 1910. In the distance can be seen the Port of Blyth Steam Fishing & Ice Company's ice house, which later during both world wars was used as torpedo stores for HMS *Elfin*, the submarine base at Blyth.

Blyth Beach, 1968. The swings belonged to Isabella Cambell Cooper, Nanny Cooper to her grandchildren, Madame Stella to her circus friends and the Lady with the swings to the children that played on the beach.

The Mermaid Cafe, Links Road, Blyth, June 1968. It was built as the Jubilee Cafe to mark the jubilee year of King George V in 1935.

One of the many annual gatherings of Sunday school children on the 'Flatts' at the south end of Bath Terrace, *c.* 1910.

A well known Blyth man Mr Martino, *c.* 1960. During the summer he would be seen with his ice cream barrow and in the winter he would be out and about with his hot chestnut barrow.

Originally the Flatts and part of the Links, the area was landscaped and opened as Ridley Park on the 27 July 1904.

A winter scene looking across the Rose Garden in Ridley Park, 1962. This was shortly after the band stand had been removed and a rose garden was being constructed on the site.

A Jazz Band Contest at Blyth, 22 August 1962. The band is marching from Regent Street into Waterloo Road.

Morris Dancers at Blyth Bus Station on the 22 September 1962.

From 1924 to 1938 each year in September there was a Carnival Day held to raise funds in aid of the Thomas Knight Memorial Hospital.

All dressed and ready to take part in the Blyth Carnival on the 7 September 1929. Left to right: Ralph Taylor, Billy Laidlaw and son, with Edna Patten and Gladys Hewitson in front of them, Tom Carlisle as the Policeman, Joe Fulbeck, George Hewitson, Alf Terry (?), the last person is unknown.

Excitement mounting as the pupils from Newlands School (now Ridley High) wait on the platform at Newsham Station for the train to take them on their annual school trip, 3 July 1967. The station was opened specially for the occasion.

Travelling hoppings in the forecourt of the old railway station, 15 November 1967. Safeway's store is now on this site.

William Tudor, Circus Proprietor. He built his first circus in Croft Road in April 1892. His next circus was the Hippodrome in Union Street which opened on Monday 10 March 1902. He converted the skating rink in Post Office Square into the second Hippodrome during February 1920. He was also the first person to bring moving pictures to Blyth. He died aged eighty-seven on the 20 August 1940.

Edith and William Tudor with some of their ponies in their act at the first Hippodrome. The ponies were purchased from the Seaton Delaval Coal Company. The site of this circus is where the Wallaw Cinema now stands.

Originally a roller skating rink it was converted into the Hippodrome Cinema and opened on the 6 March 1920. It was later rebuilt as the Roxy Cinema and Ballroom.

The Roxy, still known to some of the older generations of Blyth as Tudor's Ballroom. The building is now a bingo hall.

The first Theatre Royal, built after the Octagon Theatre was burnt down in 1875. It became the Alexandria Hall in 1901. It later became a billiards hall and was demolished in the late 1980s to make way for the Keel Row shopping mall.

The second Theatre Royal, built in 1900, was managed by Arthur Jefferson, the father of Stan Laurel. It closed as a theatre on the 28 February 1959 and demolished in the 1970s after being a workshop for a number of years.

The Central Cinema in the Market Place, *c*. 1930. Blyth's first talkie cinema closed as a cinema in June 1961 to become the town's first full-time bingo hall.

Central Cinema, 14 October 1964. It was closed as a bingo hall and stood empty for more than ten years before being demolished. Formerly the Central Hall it was built in 1858 and rebuilt after a fire in 1923 as a cinema.

Cowpen Colliery Brass Band, *c.* 1900. Like many of the other local brass bands they would give concerts from the band stand in Ridley Park on Sunday evenings during the summer.

Bolckow's United FC, 1920-21. Like many industries in Blyth at the beginning of the twentieth century Bolckow's the shipbreakers had their own football team, but like many such photographs we do not know the names of the players.

Blyth Spartans Ladies football team, 1918-19. They were the first Blyth women's team to play competitive football, playing their home games at Croft Park.

Blyth St Mary's football team, 1926-27. Runners-up to New Hartley Templars in the Blyth & District Church League.

Blyth Rowing Club members, c. 1900, in front of their club house, near Greenland Row, Cowpen Square. This club and another based at the Golden Fleece, amalgamated in 1906 with the Golden Fleece as their headquarters.

Blyth Rowing Club, winners of the professional four-oared race at Durham Regatta, 1909. Crew: J. Luke (bow), J. Charlton (2nd), J. Lavery (3rd), C. Allen (stroke), W. Hickey (cox).

A famous rowing family at Blyth, all members of Blyth Rowing Club. Left to right: Jack Allen (father), Thomas S. Allen (son), Cornelius Allen (grandfather). This photograph shows all the trophies won by Thomas Steel Allen in the 1956 season.

Members of the Blyth Rowing Club who won the Junior-Senior event at South Hylton Regatta, Sunderland, 22 May 1967. They beat Chester-le-Street in the semi-final and Cambois in the final. Left to right: C. Gotts, J. Liddle, A. Railton, and T.S. Allen (stroke).

At one time the local pub was the equivalent to the present day community centre, holding sporting and social events. The above picture shows a local cricket team in front of the old Market Inn, Waterloo, *c.* 1900.

Blyth & District Cycling Club, 1929, outside their headquarters at the Central Hall at Blyth Market Place.

Four

Transport

This picture shows the first chain High Ferry at the Cowpen Square landing. This steam ferry service started in 1890. In the background are the buildings of the Golden Fleece and the houses of Cowpen Square, *c.* 1900.

In 1924 new ferry boats came into service which had some accommodation for foot passengers. This picture shows the High Ferry during the latter half of the 1950s.

The last day in service for the old chain ferry at Blyth, Tuesday 30 June 1964. This was replaced the next day by the motor passenger ferry BHC No. 5.

A steam passenger train leaving Blyth. Cowpen Road Gates and signal box are in the background with Harper Street on the right.

The railway station on Turner Street was built in 1895 and continued in use until it came under the Beeching axe in 1964. The picture shows the station on the 12 August 1964 shortly before it was closed down.

The last passenger train to leave Blyth Railway Station on the 12 August 1964.

A Land Rover fitted for travelling on railway tracks, standing in Blyth Station, 29 November 1965. The vehicle was used by the company that was removing the tracks.

The disused station at Blyth stood derelict for many years. This part of the site is now covered by Safeway's store and car park. While the western end now has the Community Hospital and Health Centre on it.

This view taken from the railway bridge in April 1966 shows the station forecourt with the little Maynard's tobacconists shop and Turner Street down to the Market Place corner.

In the days before the steam or motor vehicle, most commercial transport was one horse power. Vehicles like T. York's butchers cart probably changed very little in style over 150 years. I can remember a butchers cart like this one being in use until the mid 1950s.

During the late 1930s and '40s a regular scene around the streets of Blyth was Bell's horse drawn ice cream cart, seen here in Balfour Street just after leaving their factory in Goschen Street, Cowpen Quay.

Thompson's horse drawn box cart used for furniture removals. Jane Thompson & Sons were haulage contractors using both horse and motor wagons. The company was formed just after the First World War and continued until 1966 when the last of the sons died.

J. Thompson & Sons' main building and yard was in Princess Louise Road, between Croft Road and Coomassie Road. The unusual feature of the main building was on the ground floor were the offices and garage, while on the first floor was the stables. The horses having to walk or gallop up a wood ramp to get to their stalls.

There is mention of horse drawn omnibuses at Blyth in the mid nineteenth century, but it is not until the 1920s before there is any mention of Blyth Bus Station. This photograph shows what it looked like in the mid 1930s.

The T. & B. fleet of Bedford buses, November 1960. Thompson & Bowman started their garage and fleet of hire cars and buses just after the First World War. Their garage was at the top of Union Street, between the Bus Station and the Theatre Royal. The business was run by Thompson's son Peter, until the area was compulsory purchased to make way for the Keel Row shopping mall.

Five

Life Saving

The *John Anthony*, Blyth No. 2 Station, 1901-1915, known locally as the Cambois Lifeboat.

The *Dash*, Blyth No. 1 Station, 1902-1921. Blyth's rowing lifeboat, with the crew in front of the Boat House in the South Harbour.

The *Dash* being launched from the slipway in the South Harbour. Note the ten oarsmen. This must be only a training exercise as none of them seem to have on the cork life preservers.

John William Bushell – b. 1875 d. in
September 1936. He was the coxswain
of the Blyth lifeboat at twenty-four years
of age. Honoured by three kings, he was
coxswain of the rowing lifeboats *Dalmar*
and the *Dash*. He brought the motor
lifeboat *Joseph Adlam* from Cowes in 1922
and served as coxswain in her until a few
years before his death.

The *Joseph Adlam* being launched from
the new lifeboat house after her naming
ceremony, Saturday 13 May 1922.

The Blyth lifeboat *Winston Churchill* being launched on a training exercise on the 20 February 1963.

The new high speed off-shore lifeboat *Windsor Runner* (Civil Service No. 42) now based at Blyth, Sunday 10 December 1995.

The Carnegie Gold Medal, presented posthumously to George Hurrel a member of the Blyth Volunteer Life Saving Company, who lost his life at the wreck of the steamer *Dunelm* at North Blyth on the 11 January 1913.

Driven on to Blyth Beach on the 20 January 1937 the steamer *Therese* was on the beach for fifty-one days before being refloated on the 12 March.

The steamer *Devonbrook* wrecked alongside the East Pier at Blyth on the 28 August 1946.

A member of the crew of the steamer *Holderness* being rescued by Breeches Buoy by the Blyth Volunteer Life Saving Company on the morning of the 11 March 1959.

The remains of the *Holderness* driven against the East Pier after the gale.

From left to right: Eddy Rolt, Dave Turnbull (Officer in Charge), Tom Davis and Bob Balmer; some of the members of the Blyth Volunteer Life Saving Company with the Chronicle Cup and the Elizabethan Trophy the Company had won in 1973.

The Blyth Fire Brigade horse drawn steam pump standing in front of the Council Offices in Seaforth Street, *c.* 1914.

Captain Fred Naisbitt sitting proudly in his new motor fire engine outside the Seaforth Street Fire Station, 29 March 1923. This new piece of equipment had just arrived from the makers in Glasgow.

The scene of devastation on Waterloo Road, opposite the Market Place and the Central Hall, after nine business premises and three offices had been destroyed by fire, 16 October 1904. The value of the loss being set at £30,000.

This fire started on 26 October 1904 in Wallace's drapery shop in Seaforth Street which was between Chisholm's large shop on Tuner Street and the Maypole Butter Company's store. At the height of the blaze all three businesses were just a roaring inferno which left nothing standing.

The first crews to be based at the Union Street Fire Station which was opened on the 17 May 1924 and consisted of a three machine engine room and two houses for the officers.

On Wednesday 16 August 1939, at 11.20 am the old Fish Market in the South Harbour was found to be on fire. The Blyth Fire Brigade, the Harbour Commission Fire Brigade, the fire tug *John Dent* and two other tugs were used to fight the fire, as well as a large number of auxiliary firemen. A large amount of damage was done and it was well into the evening before the fire was out.

By around 1960 the Blyth Fire Brigade was a two pump station. The machine in the picture is a pump escape, the other machine being a water tender. The Union Street Station closed in April 1987 when the new station on Cowpen Road was completed.

The remains of Harold Blakeborough's tobacconists shop on the Market Place corner, Saturday 23 October 1965. The fire started in a box of fireworks which had rockets, bangers and jumping crackers exploding in the shop during the blaze.

The blazing three-storey factory building of the Carobel Manufacturing Company in Quay Road, Sunday 22 September 1968. At the height of the fire flames were shooting forty feet high from the top floor of the building.

The burnt out shell of the Bebside Memorial Hall and Welfare Social Club, Saturday 14 March 1970. Firemen from Blyth, Ashington, Morpeth and Whitley Bay worked throughout the early hours of Saturday morning to control the blaze.

Six

The Port of Blyth

Looking down river and across the West Basin from one of the chimney's of Blyth Power Station, c. 1960. As can be seen, this was before the Grain Berth was built next to Battleship Wharf.

Unloading timber with steam cranes in the South Harbour, c. 1900. The sailing vessel in the background seems to be unloading pit props, probably from one of the Baltic ports.

The Rose Line Shipping Company of Sunderland and Blyth. Warehousing sugar in bags at Blyth Import Dock in 1920.

The drilling craft working near the North Blyth Staithes, *c.* 1925. As this part of the river bed is solid rock from time to time it needed to be blasted. This craft was used to drill the holes for the charges.

BHC *Rockbreaker* No. 2 built in 1907 by the Blyth Shipbuilding & Dry Dock Co. It was built on a towing barge and used to break the river bed rock so the bucket dredger could pick it up. She was owned by the Commissioners from 1907 until July 1971 when sold for scrap.

The steel bucket dredger *Cambois*, built by Flemming & Ferguson Ltd, Paisley, Scotland in 1895. It was owned by Blyth Harbour Commissioners from 1895 until May 1917 when they sold her to London owners.

The wood steam Harbour Masters launch *Cambois*. Built by Philip & Son Ltd, Dartmouth, as the *Spurn*. She was purchased by the Harbour Commission in April 1931 and in July changed her name to *Cambois*. The craft was broken up during February 1962.

A regular sight on the river was the waterboat, built in 1922 by Wood, Skinner & Co. at Bill Quay, on the Tyne. She was owned by the Harbour Commissioners from December 1922 until August 1971 when she was sold for scrap.

The steam bucket dredger *Cowpen* built in 1913 by Ferguson Bros Ltd, Port Glasgow. When built she was the largest dredger of the day. Owned by the Harbour Commissioners from 1913 until April 1964 when she was sold to Italian owners. This picture shows the *Cowpen* leaving Blyth for Palermo on the 19 May 1964.

The steam paddle tug *Steel*, built in 1889 by J.T. Eltringham at South Shields. She was purchased by the Blyth Tug Co. in September 1932 and scrapped at Hughes Bolckow Ltd, May 1958.

The steam paddle tug *Earl of Beaconsfield*, built by J.P. Rennoldson at South Shields and completed in February 1877. Purchased by George Dinsdale June 1887, she was scrapped in 1913 by Bolckow's. There was another tug of the same name at Blyth from 1922 to 1958 which was built as the *Salt* in 1889.

The steam screw tug *Homer*, built by
Ardrossan Drydock & Shipbuilding Co. Ltd,
Scotland and completed in March 1915.
She served as an armed tug between 1915-19
and sank a German submarine. She was at
Blyth from December 1958 until scrapped at
Bolckow's in March 1968.

The steam screw tug *Langton*, built by
McKnight & Co., Ayr, Scotland and
completed in November 1892. She was based
at Blyth from 1953 to 1962 when she was
laid up. Blyth crew, left to right: J. Little,
C. Aynsley, B. Moss, the boy is unknown.
Isaac Black with J. Wood in front of him, and
Chris Clark the skipper.

The steam twin screw fire fighting tug *Chipchase*, launched from Clelands Ltd yard at Wallsend on the 17 April 1953 and handed over to the Harbour Commissioners on the 24 June 1953 having cost £55,775 to build. Capt. E. Parks followed by Jack Barrett were the only two masters she had during her fifteen years at Blyth.

On the 8 July 1964 the *Chipchase* was involved in an accident with the collier *Blackwall Point* from which she sank. After nineteen days on the river bed she was raised and put into No. 4 dry dock and repaired. She worked at Blyth until 1968 when she left to become the harbour tug at Seaham Harbour, County Durham.

The steam screw tug *Seasider*, built by Crabtree & Co. Ltd at Great Yarmouth and completed as the *West Hyde*, July 1919. She was renamed *Seasider* in 1948 and was based at Blyth from September 1949 until scrapped at Bolckow's in March 1969.

The motor screw tug *Maximus*, the last tug to be based at Blyth. Built at Cuxhaven, Germany and completed in March 1956, she was sold to the Blyth Tug Co. in May 1971. The ownership passed to Lawson-Batey Tugs Ltd in March 1978, but she remained at Blyth. With the decline in trade at Blyth she was laid up at Sunderland in December 1983 and was sold in January of the following year.

HMS *Vulcan*, Submarine Depot Ship in the South Harbour with some of the submarines of the 14th Flotilla which were based at Blyth during the First World War. Another depot ship that was also based at Blyth at this time was HMS *Titania*.

The Second World War British submarine *Tally Ho* at Blyth in early 1945 for a refit after returning from an East Indies patrol.

The Dutch submarine *Tijgerhaai*, leaving the port after a visit during February 1960. Built by Vickers-Armstrong at Barrow as HMS *Tarn*, she was launched during November 1944, completed 6 April 1945 and later sold to the Royal Dutch Navy.

The British submarine *Oracle* lying at the Dun Cow Quay, while visiting Blyth, 21 January 1966. Built by Cammell Laird & Co. Ltd at Birkenhead, she was launched during September 1961 and completed on the 14 February 1963.

One of the Dutch suction dredgers lying at the Dun Cow Quay while working at Blyth on the Alcan Project, 21 February 1970.

The completed Alcan Terminal, built between 1969 and 1971, on the site where the old Cowpen Coal Company Staithes had been. The first cargo of 5,000 tons of alumina for Alcan arrived on the 29 June 1971.

Seven

The Coal Trade

Bebside Colliery, Horton Grange Pit. The main shaft was sunk in 1853 and continued working until it ceased coal working on the 26 January 1962.

Crofton Mill Pit's shaft was sunk in 1885. Coal working ceased at the pit on the 12 July 1969. This pit was the closest to the town centre being on the south side of Plessey Road opposite Union Street.

Miss Polly Jones, manageress at Crofton Mill Pit canteen for twenty years, on her last day at work on the 9 September 1969.

Cowpen Isabella Colliery, known locally as the 'Bella Pit', was opened in 1848. The Straker shaft was sunk in 1874 and coal working ceased here on the 12 February 1966.

The houses may have been called New Row, at Isabella Colliery but 'New' was during 1870s. Before that date there were no houses at the 'Bella', the miners living at Cowpen Colliery. This picture shows the houses in August 1961.

Bates Colliery as it was on the 15 February 1960. Cowpen 'B' Pit, sunk in 1804, became part of Bates Pit in 1923. In January 1961 the new shaft was taken down to a depth of 1,000 feet. Coal working ceased at Bates on the 31 May 1986.

During the modernisation of Bates from 1960-61 the water tower for the coal cleaning plant was demolished on the 24 February 1961.

Vessels waiting to load coal in 1934 at the newly completed Cowpen South Staiths, locally known as Bates loading point.

The Sunderland built *Lord Citrine* loading at Bates loading point, 6 December 1961. Built by Wm Pickersgill & Sons Ltd in 1950, she was scrapped in 1972 at Bo'ness.

One of the many teams of North Eastern Railway trimmers at Blyth. This photo was taken onboard the steamship *Fountains Abbey* in 1906.

The *Ferryhill, c.* 1960. This was the second vessel of the same name owned by the Aberdeen Coal & Shipping Co. Ltd – regular traders out of Blyth over a period of fifty years. The first *Ferryhill* was mined in Blyth Bay while leaving the port on the 21 January 1940.

South Blyth, North Eastern Railway Staiths, *c.* 1930. Following various improvements from the river's first staith in 1788 the main extensions were undertaken in 1888.

South Blyth N.E.R. Staiths, 10 May 1966. They were closed down at the same time as the railway in 1964 and work started during the summer of 1966 on their demolition.

The coal bunkering berth on the High Quay, c. 1920. This was the coal loading staith used by the steam tugs and trawlers at Blyth.

The N.E.R. West Staithes. The substructure was completed in 1915, but the superstructure was not completed until 1926 and it was another two years before the first shipment of coal was loaded here. These staiths were demolished in 1996.

Cowpen Coal Company Staiths at North Blyth, *c.* 1880, as they were when first built in 1868 before they were set back and the river straightened up and made deeper in the 1890s.

Cowpen Coal Company Staiths at North Blyth with the collier *Cormist* having just finished loading, 4 July 1966. These staiths closed in 1968 and were demolished for the building of the Alcan Terminal.

Steam colliers laid up at both sides of the middle jetty in the South Harbour, while waiting to go up river to load coal, Tuesday 21 January 1964.

The steam collier *Borde* passing up river to load coal, 21 January 1966. Note the two foymen in the small launch running up to get ahead of the collier to take the lines ashore.

The 2,200 ton collier *Greenland*, 26 May 1966. She was 'blacked' by the National Union of Seamen as she lay strikebound in the South Harbour after having been sailed north by her officers.

N.E.R. North Blyth Staiths, *c.* 1960. Formally opened on the 13 July 1896, the first vessel loaded was the steamer *Woodhorn*. These staiths were demolished in 1972.

N.E.R. North Blyth Staiths, *c.* 1972. A view along the top of the staiths just before demolition work started. The large grab crane at the Alcan Berth can be seen in the background.

North Blyth Staiths, *c.* 1972 while demolition work was in progress. It is plain to see how much timber was used in the building of the staiths. Most of the timber was pitch pine with greenhart for the underwater piles.

Eight

Other Industries

This is the only sketch showing the first dry dock at Blyth. Built in 1811 by Linskill & Holland, this dock was enlarged in the 1880s and later became No. 4 dock, which still exists today.

The plate handling gang at Blyth Shipbuilding & Dry Dock Co. Ltd, *c.* 1910. It was the job of this gang of men with their steam crane to take steel plates from the plate stores to the plating shop where they were shaped for the hull of a ship.

A forest of steel uprights with a vessel slowly taking shape among them. This picture shows a vessel under construction on one of the five building berths at Blyth Shipyard.

HMS *Barbarian* being launched on Thursday 21 October 1937. This was the first of twenty-four boom defence vessels built at Blyth spread over a period of three years. There were seventeen 750 ton 'Bar' class vessels and seven 456 ton 'Net' class vessels.

HMS *Cawsand Bay*, laid down as HMS *Loch Roan* but launched as *Cawsand Bay* on the 20 February 1945. She was completed at Hughes Bolckow's who during the war were ship fitters not breakers. After serving in the Royal Navy and the Reserve Fleet she was scrapped in 1959 at Genoa, Italy.

One of the largest war-damage repairs was the rebuilding of the tanker *Erodona*. Torpedoed in the North Atlantic on the 15 March 1941 about one-third of the stern end was blown off. The remaining part of the vessel was towed to England were it discharged the petrol cargo that was left.

In 1943 due to the shortage of tankers the hulk was towed to Blyth, the damaged parts removed at Bolckow's. In 1944 she was put into No. 3 dry dock were a new stern half was built on, from just aft of the bridge. The *Erodona* returned to service just before the end of the war in 1945.

Seven female tack welders employed at Blyth Shipyard in 1964. Women had been employed in the shipyard at Blyth from 1941 in such jobs as welders, burners, crane drivers and bench fitters, as well as a wide range of other jobs.

Mrs Annie Elliott a tack welder at Blyth Shipyard, 1964. During the war years there were thirty women employed in the shipyard, but they were paid off at the end of the war. Due to the shortage of male welders some women were taken on again and were there until the yard closed in 1966.

Isaac Carter 5,626 ton Newsprint Carrier, launched Thursday 8 May 1952 at Blyth and completed during September 1952. She was owned by Barberry S.S. Co. of London from 1952 to 1964 when sold and renamed *North America*. After an engine room explosion on the 23 June 1968 she was scrapped in Japan in 1969.

Harpalycus 7,562 ton motor vessel built at Blyth in 1959 for the National S.S. Co. Ltd of London. The vessel was lengthened in 1968 which gave her a tonnage of 10,212 tons. She was sold in 1975 and renamed *Filikos* and again changed names in 1980 to *Sabrina*. The vessel was not listed in 1984.

The *Chapel River* nearly ready for launching early in May 1962. At this stage the bows would be towering above the traffic at the top end of Regent Street.

Motor Bulk Carrier *Chapel River*, 16,398 tons, completed September 1962 and owned by the River Line Ltd of London from 1962 to 1970. The vessel was named *Corconado* from 1970 to 1973. For a short period in 1973 she was named *Ipanema* and then sold to the People's Republic of China and renamed *Qing Hai*. After that her fate is unknown.

Motor Vessel *Corchester*, 4,840 tons, completed for Cory Maritime Ltd of London during March 1965. The vessel was transferred to the Liquid Gas Tanker Ltd (managed by Cory) in 1970 and sold by them in 1977 to the Central Electricity Generating Board.

Dolphin Point, ex *Corchester*, berthing at Blyth in 1985. Purchased by the C.E.G.B. in 1977 and renamed *Dolphin Point* she was a regular visitor to Blyth until laid up at West Hartlepool during 1986 and sold in 1987.

At 3.30 on Thursday afternoon the 11 June 1953 in fifty-four seconds the hull of the 12,624 ton motor tanker *William G. Walkley* was launched into the river. She was completed and handed over to AMPOL Petroleum Ltd of Sidney, Australia on the 17 February 1954.

The 4,997 ton motor collier *Rogate*, the last vessel to be built at the yard of the Blyth Dry Dock & Shipbuilding Co. Ltd. She was launched by Charles Long a shipyard employee on Thursday 24 November 1966. Only having one owner, Stephenson Clark Shipping, she last sailed from Blyth on the 3 March 1986. She was laid up in April and sold for scrap in June 1986.

The history of the ship's figurehead of the Greek goddess Ceres, which was outside the offices of Hughes Bolckow Ltd, was said to be over 200 year old. Here she is on 23 June 1970. Where she came from originally is lost in the mists of time, but she is thought to have come to North Blyth when the company started here in 1911.

U-boats in the tidal dock, 1919

After the First World War six German submarines were brought to Battleship Wharf for breaking up. They were the U19, U22, U30, U33, U35 and the U98. There was some excitement when U98 arrived at Blyth as she came into collision with the West Pier causing some damage.

A view of Hughes Bolckow's yard at North Blyth. This shot was taken from a vessel at the main quay with the stern half of a vessel on the tidal slipway being cut up and lifted ashore by the derricks and a steam crane.

The 14,100 ton cruiser HMS *Leviathan* stripped down to deck level, *c*. 1920. Built in 1901, she was the flagship for North America and the West Indies, 1915-18. The 13,590 ton Cruiser HMS *Duke of Edinburgh* can be seen waiting to come to Battleship Wharf.

A view of the main deck of HMS *Thunderer* as she arrived at Blyth for the second time on the 14 April 1927. The gun turrets had been removed to lighten the vessel as she had grounded at the first attempt to get into Blyth.

On Thursday 4 December 1930 the Canadian Pacific Liner *Empress of Scotland* arrived at Blyth to be broken up by Hughes Bolckow at Battleship Wharf after having paid £43,000 for the vessel.

At 4.00 am on Wednesday 10 December 1930 the *Empress of Scotland* was found to be on fire. More than 100 firemen fought the blaze without success. Thousands of people came to both sides of the river during the next four days to watch the great liner burn.

BATTLESHIP TEAKWOOD
GARDEN FURNITURE

Estimates free for any design and size of
Garden Trellis, Pergolas, Rose Bowers, etc.

The Hughes Bolckow Shipbreaking Co. Ltd.

Manufacturers of Garden Furniture from the Teakwood of Battleships

BATTLESHIP WHARF, BLYTH, NORTHUMBERLAND

Telephone - Blyth 25. Telegrams: "Battleships, Blyth"

Fully illustrated Catalogue of Garden Seats, Tables, Tea Wagons, etc.,
sent free on request.

This 1930s advert shows what some of the timber from the scrapped vessels was used for.

The 10,689 ton tanker *Tectus*, built in 1945 by the Alabama Dry Dock & Shipbuilding Co. as the *Crow Wing*. In 1947 she was renamed *Tectus*. This picture shows her being scrapped at North Blyth in 1961.

The Battle Class Destroyer HMS *Alamein* arriving at Blyth for scrapping in February 1964. The 2,000 ton vessel had been built by Hawthorn, Leslie & Co. at Hebburn in 1945.

The Royal Navy Reserve, Tyne Drill Ship HMS *Calliope* arriving at Blyth for scrapping at North Blyth near the end of April 1968.

The 7,000 ton Canadian built liberty ship *Santagata* at Battleship Wharf for scrapping, 30 January 1971. Built in 1944, she spent most of her working life with the Elder Dempster Line.

With the new diesel locomotives coming into use a large number of redundant steam locomotives went onto the scrap market. These are some of the locomotives scrapped by Bolckow's at North Blyth, September 1964.

Blyth & Cowpen Gas Company situated behind Bridge Street was formed in 1852. The gas works were enlarged and brought up to date between 1912-14. The gas industry was nationalised in May 1949 and the Blyth Gas Works were again modernised between 1950-53.

During March 1920 John B. Bilton & Co. Ltd took over the engineering business of G. Maughan at 3 Plessey Road, Blyth. This photograph shows some of the staff in 1954. Left to right: J. Jones, R. Spence, G. Hogg, H. Garrod, W. Wilson, J. Thompson, P. Rae and G. Fulcher. The works closed down in November 1973.

A steam herring drifter heading out of Blyth to hunt the 'Silver Shoals', *c.* 1910.

Blyth Fish Quay with some of the herring fleet unloading their catch, *c.* 1914. One or two of these vessels were owned by the Port Of Blyth Steam Fishing & Ice Company.

126

As the Scottish herring fleet moved down the east coast upwards of 600 women from the northern Scottish ports moved from port to port gutting and packing into barrels the herring that were caught.

The Blyth coble *Rejoice* up on the quay for an overhaul in the late 1930s. The painters are Tom Fawcus painting the waterline, while Bob Watson the owner/skipper paints the gunnel.

Blyth 'A' and 'B' Power Stations looking across from the road down to Factory Point at Cowpen.

Blyth 'A' Power Station looking down from one of the chimneys of the 'B' Station.